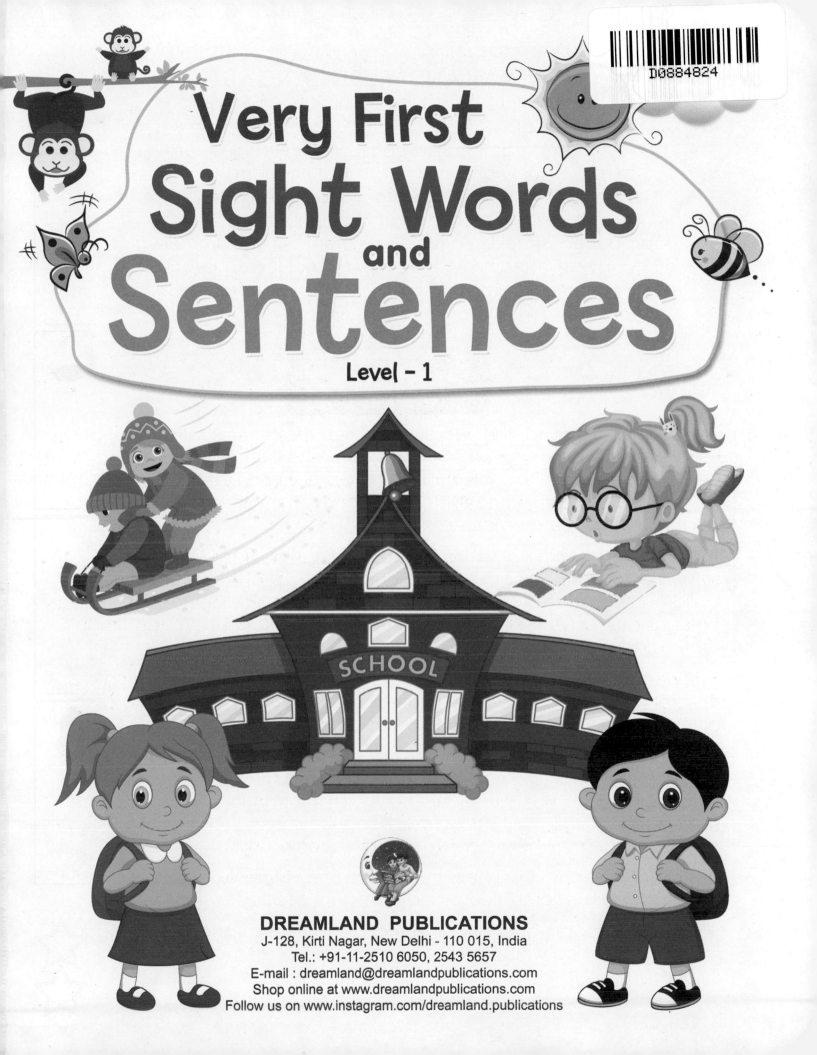

Very First
Sight Words
and
Sentences

Level - 1

DREAMLAND PUBLICATIONS

J-128, Kirti Nagar, New Delhi - 110 015, India

Tel.: +91-11-2510 6050, 2543 5657

E-mail : dreamland@dreamlandpublications.com

Shop online at www.dreamlandpublications.com

Follow us on www.instagram.com/dreamland.publications

Published in 2022 by
DREAMLAND PUBLICATIONS
J-128, Kirti Nagar, New Delhi - 110 015, India
Tel : +91-11-2510 6050, 2543 5657
E-mail : dreamland@dreamlandpublications.com
www.dreamlandpublications.com

Preface

Sight words refer to the words that are most frequently used and repeated in any text. These words are also sometimes referred to as "high-frequency" words that are most commonly found in written language. Although some fit standard phonetic patterns, some do not and they must be memorised.

There are approximately 13 words (a, and, for, he, is, in, it, of, that, the, to, was, you) that account for more than 25% of the words in print. Children see these words all around them every day. They see them on signs and advertisements, on the walls of their classrooms and many other places.

The present set – Very First Sight Words and Sentences – is meant for children of age-group 4+ which corresponds to Nursery and KG standards of the primary schools. It contains top sight words that a child will be studying throughout the year and some additional enrichment words.

Each sight word is followed by a sentence using the word. The sentence is to help the child figure out the word through the context of the sentence. This will help the child recognise these words immediately and read them without having to use decoding skills.

This set of two books will help the children read the text easily and they will gradually become fluent and confident readers.

Suggestions for bringing about any improvement for the betterment of the books shall be welcomed to be incorporated in the coming editions if found up to the mark.

Contents

I

I sleep.

I skate.

I swim.

I eat.

I run.

I read.

I paint.

Colour a star each time you read each sentence.

I dance.

I sing.

I drink.

I play.

I write.

I pray.

I help.

I jump.

Colour a star each time you read each sentence.

like

I like pizza.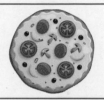

I like bananas.

I like apples.

I like eggs.

I like carrots.

I like cookies.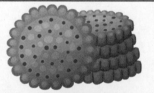

I like cake.

Colour a star each time you read each sentence.

I like chocolate.

I like ice cream.

I like cherries.

I like oranges.

I like mango.

I like milk.

I like sandwiches.

I like grapes.

Colour a star each time you read each sentence.

my

I like my dog.

I like my cat.

I like my fish.

I like my ball.

I like my car.

I like my airplane.

I like my books.

Colour a star each time you read each sentence.

I like my toys.

I like my friends.

I like my bag.

I like my school.

I like my teddy bear.

I like my cap.

I like my bed.

I like my uniform.

Colour a star each time you read each sentence.

see

I see my dog.

I like my dog.

I see my cat.

I like my cat.

I see my fish.

I like my fish.

I like my pets.

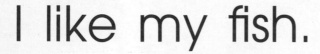

Colour a star each time you read each sentence.

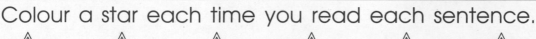

I see my bat.

I like my bat.

I see my bag.

I like my bag.

I see my toys.

I like my toys.

I see my car.

I like my car.

Colour a star each time you read each sentence.

can

I can see my ball.

I like my ball.

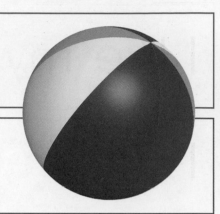

I can see my duck.

I like my duck.

I can see my blocks.

I like my blocks.

I like my toys.

Colour a star each time you read each sentence.

I can see my bag.

I like my bag.

I can see my books.

I like my books.

I can see my hat.

I like my hat.

I can see my bicycle.

I like my bicycle.

Colour a star each time you read each sentence.

the

I can see the dog.

I like the dog.

I see the cat.

I like the cat.

I can see the fish.

I like the fish.

The fish can swim.

Colour a star each time you read each sentence.

I can see the stars.

I like the stars.

I can see the flowers.

I like the flowers.

I can see the butterfly.

I like the butterfly.

I can see the rainbow.

I like the rainbow.

Colour a star each time you read each sentence.

go

I see the bus.

The bus can go.

I can see the car.

The car can go.

I see my bike.

My bike can go.

I like my bike.

Colour a star each time you read each sentence.

a

I can see a hat.

I like the hat.

I see a balloon.

I like the balloon.

I can see a cake.

I like the cake.

Colour a star each time you read each sentence.

to

I can swim.
I like to swim.

I can paint.
I like to paint.

I can run.
I like to run.

I can read.
I like to read.

Colour a star each time you read each sentence.

we

We can see a slide.
We like to slide.

We see the swings.
We like to swing.

We can see a pizza.
We like to eat pizza.

Colour a star each time you read each sentence.

you

Can you see
the farm?

I can see the cows.
Can you see
the cows?

I can see the tractor.
Can you see
the tractor?

I like to go
to the farm.

Colour a star each time you read each sentence.

look

Look at the pumpkins. I can see 3 pumpkins.

Look at the cats. I can see 4 cats.

Look at the bats. I can see 5 bats.

Look at the ghost. **Boo!**

Colour a star each time you read each sentence.

at

"Look at my dog," said the girl.

"Look at my cat," said the boy.

"Look at the bees," said Mom.

Look at us go!

Colour a star each time you read each sentence.

big

I like to go
to the zoo.

I can see a big
elephant. Can
you see the big
elephant?

I can see a big
giraffe. Can
you see the
big giraffe?

Colour a star each time you read each sentence.

is

We see the barn.
The barn is big.

I can see a horse.
The horse is big.

We can see a cow.
The cow is big.

I can see a fly.
Is the fly big?

Colour a star each time you read each sentence.

with

The cat is with the dog.

The horse is with the cow.

The frog is with the turtle.

The boy is with the girl.

Colour a star each time you read each sentence.

for

The bone is
for the dog.

The carrot is
for the rabbit.

The grass is for
the cow.

The apple is for
the girl.

Colour a star each time you read each sentence.

he

He is painting.

He is eating.

He is swimming.

He is skating.

He is running.

He is reading.

He is sleeping.

Colour a star each time you read each sentence.

she

She is painting.
She likes to paint.

She is skating.
She likes to skate.

She is riding a cycle.
She likes to ride a cycle.

She is reading.
She loves to read!

Colour a star each time you read each sentence.

little

I can see a mouse.
The mouse is little.

I can see a frog.
The frog is little.

I can see a duck.
The duck is little.

I can see a horse.
Is the horse little?

Colour a star each time you read each sentence.

have

I have a bike.
My bike is big.

I have a ball.
My ball is big.

I have a dog.
My dog is big.

I have a fish.
Is the fish big?

Colour a star each time you read each sentence.

here

I can see snow!

Here is my hat.

Here is my jacket.

Here is my friend.

Here is a snowman.

Here is the sled.
Here we go!

Colour a star each time you read each sentence.

are

We can go to the farm!

Here are the cows.

Here are the horses.

Here are the goats.

Here are the ducks.

We like the farm!

Colour a star each time you read each sentence.

and

I can see apples and bananas.
I like apples and bananas.

I can see cherries and oranges.
I like cherries and oranges.

I like fruit!

Colour a star each time you read each sentence.

play

He likes to play with the big truck.

She likes to play with the ball.

He likes to play with the blocks.

My dog likes to play with me.

Colour a star each time you read each sentence.

said

He said, "I have a dog. My dog is big. I like to play with my dog."

She said, "I have a little cat. My cat likes to play with the ball."

He said, "I have a horse. My horse is big. I can ride on my horse."

Colour a star each time you read each sentence.

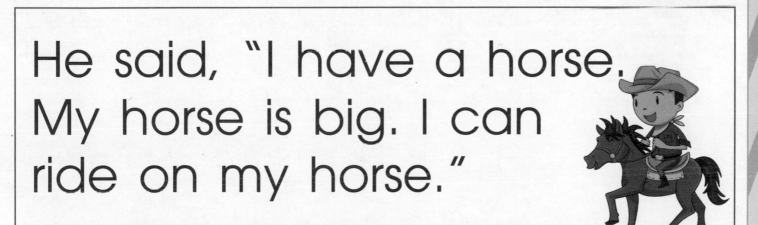

put

Tom said, "Can I go out to play?"

Mom said, "Put on your boots."

Dad said, "Get your coat and put it on."

Mom said, "Put on your hat and mittens."

Tom put on his boots, coat, hat and mittens. He ran out to play in the snow.

Colour a star each time you read each sentence.

come

"I like to swing," said the girl, "Come and swing with me."

"I like to skate," said the girl, "Come and skate with me."

"We like to play," said the boys and girls, "Come and play with us."

Colour a star each time you read each sentence.

they

I can see two girls.
They like to play soccer.

I see three boys. They
like to play basketball.

I see a boy and a
girl. They like to go
bowling.

They all like to go
for ice cream.

Colour a star each time you read each sentence.

this

This boy has a wagon.
He likes his wagon.

This girl likes to
jump rope.

This boy has a football.
He likes to play
football.

This girl has a dog.
She loves to play
with her dog.

Colour a star each time you read each sentence.

help

This boy likes to help.
He helps rake the leaves.

This boy can help. He
helps sweep the floor.

This girl can help too.
She helps feed the fish.

This girl helps. She
helps hold the door.

They can all help.

Colour a star each time you read each sentence.

in

This boy is in a little plane. He can go up in his plane.

This boy is in a boat. He likes to ride in the boat.

This boy is in a little car. He can go fast in his car.

This boy is in bed. Zzzzzzzz!

Colour a star each time you read each sentence.

me

"Look at me," said the girl, "I can skate."

"Look at me," said the boy, "I can rake the leaves."

This girl said, "Look at me. I can ride my horse."

Colour a star each time you read each sentence.

on

This boy is on a horse. He has a hat on his head. The girl is on a horse too.

This boy is on a bicycle. He has a helmet on his head. The girl is on a bicycle too. She loves to ride her bicycle.

Colour a star each time you read each sentence.

up

The sun is up in the sky.

This girl has a kite.
The kite can go up.
It can go up, up, up!

Here is a little bird.
The bird can go up.
It can go up to a
nest in the tree.

This boy is in a balloon.
The balloon can go
up, up and away!

Colour a star each time you read each sentence.

down

I can see a boy and a girl. The boy is up and the girl is down.

This girl is up and the boy is down.

This boy likes to slide. He is going down the slide.

I can see two boys. They like to sit down and play with trucks.

Colour a star each time you read each sentence.

away

I see a little boy in a balloon. He can go up, up and away!

This girl can go up in her plane. She can go up, up and away!

The helicopter can go up too. Up, up and away!

The rocket can go to the moon. Up, up and away!

Colour a star each time you read each sentence.

jump

This little frog likes to jump.

It can jump on the rock.

It can jump by the tree.

It can jump by the flowers.

It can jump on me.

Jump, frog, jump!

Colour a star each time you read each sentence.

of

We can see a lot of flowers.

We can see a lot of trees.

Here come a lot of clouds.

We can see a lot of umbrellas!

Colour a star each time you read each sentence.

where

Where is the boy?
He is on the swing.

Where is the boy?
He is by the pool.

Where is the boy?
He is on the rug.

Where is the boy?
He is in the sandbox.

Where is the boy?
He is in bed.

Colour a star each time you read each sentence.

do

The girl said, "Do you have a pet?"

The boy said, "Do you have a big dog?"

The girl said, "I do not have a big dog."

The boy said, "Do you have a little cat?"

The girl said, "I do not have a dog or a cat. I have a fish."

Colour a star each time you read each sentence.

it

It is raining. This boy likes to play in the rain.

It is sunny. This girl likes to water the flowers.

It is windy. This boy likes to fly his kite.

It is snowing. The boys like to make a snowman. The girl likes to skate. They all like to go sledding!

Colour a star each time you read each sentence.

be

It is Halloween.
What will the kids be?

This boy will be a pirate.
He will be out on Halloween.

This boy will be a ghost.
He will be out on Halloween.

This girl will be a ladybug.
She will be out on
Halloween.

They hope the bats will
not be out on Halloween!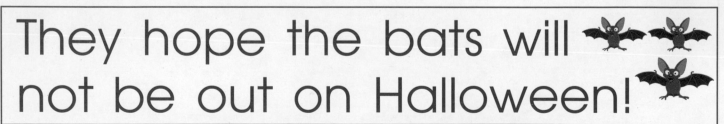

Colour a star each time you read each sentence.

52

went

The bear went over the mountain,

The bear went over the mountain.

The bear went over the mountain,

To see what he could see.

He saw a den and he went to sleep!

Colour a star each time you read each sentence.

or

Pam said, "I do not like flies or bees."

Kim said, "I do not like snails or spiders."

They said, "We do not like snakes or frogs."

Tom said, "I do not like mice or bats."

They all said, "We like butterflies!"

Colour a star each time you read each sentence.

had

Tom and Matt had fun playing soccer.

They had fun playing basketball too!

Kim and Pam had fun jumping rope.

Pam and Tom had fun on the swings.

They all had fun on the slide!

Colour a star each time you read each sentence.

but

The hen said, "I will get you!" but the cookie ran away.

The cow said, "I will get you!" but the cookie was too fast.

The man said, "Stop!" but the cookie got away.

The woman said, "Stop!" but the cookie said, "No!"

The fox said, "I will get you!" and he did.

Colour a star each time you read each sentence.

how

This girl knows how to play soccer!

The boys know how to play basketball.

That boy knows how to kick the football.

This boy knows how to jump rope.

They all know how to have fun.

Colour a star each time you read each sentence.

walk

This dog can walk and it can run.

A turtle can walk. It can swim too.

A fish can swim but it can not walk.

This bird can fly. It can walk and hop too.

A snake can slither but it can not walk.

Colour a star each time you read each sentence.

am

"I am on my bike," said Pam, "I am going to school."

"I am on my bike too," said Tom, "I can ride to school with you."

"I am walking to school," said Jim, "I like to walk to school."

Jill said, "I am walking to school too. I can walk with you."

Colour a star each time you read each sentence.

now

If you can read cow,
it helps you read now.

If you can write cow,
it helps you write now.

If you can read now,
it helps you read how.

If you can write now,
it helps you write how.

You can read now!

Colour a star each time you read each sentence.

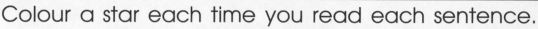

SO

This ant is so little.
The mouse is so small.

The elephant is so big.
That giraffe is so tall.

This rabbit is so fast.
That turtle is so slow.

The rabbit saw a dog,
so look at it go!

Colour a star each time you read each sentence.

into

The horses went into the barn. The lambs went into the barn. The cows went into the barn.

The farmer went into the house. The cat went into the house. The dog went into the house. Good night!

Colour a star each time you read each sentence.

an

An ant hatches from an egg.

An octopus hatches from an egg too.

An eel hatches from an egg.

An alligator hatches from an egg.

An eagle hatches from an egg too.

Colour a star each time you read each sentence.

very

Pam was very sad.
She went for a walk.

Pam saw a big bat.
She was very scared
of the bat.

The bat flew away.
It flew very fast.

Pam was very happy
that the bat was gone.

Colour a star each time you read each sentence.